AWESOME DOGS

Newfoundlands

by Nathan Sommer

BELLWETHER MEDIA • MINNEAPOLIS, MN

Note to Librarians, Teachers, and Parents:

Blastoff! Readers are carefully developed by literacy experts and combine standards-based content with developmentally appropriate text.

Level 1 provides the most support through repetition of high-frequency words, light text, predictable sentence patterns, and strong visual support.

Level 2 offers early readers a bit more challenge through varied simple sentences, increased text load, and less repetition of high-frequency words.

Level 3 advances early-fluent readers toward fluency through increased text and concept load, less reliance on visuals, longer sentences, and more literary language.

Level 4 builds reading stamina by providing more text per page, increased use of punctuation, greater variation in sentence patterns, and increasingly challenging vocabulary.

Level 5 encourages children to move from "learning to read" to "reading to learn" by providing even more text, varied writing styles, and less familiar topics.

Whichever book is right for your reader, Blastoff! Readers are the perfect books to build confidence and encourage a love of reading that will last a lifetime!

This edition first published in 2018 by Bellwether Media, Inc.

No part of this publication may be reproduced in whole or in part without written permission of the publisher. For information regarding permission, write to Bellwether Media, Inc., Attention: Permissions Department, 5357 Penn Avenue South, Minneapolis, MN 55419.

Library of Congress Cataloging-in-Publication Data

Names: Sommer, Nathan, author.
Title: Newfoundlands / by Nathan Sommer.
Description: Minneapolis, MN : Bellwether Media, Inc., [2018] | Series:
    Blastoff! Readers. Awesome Dogs | Audience: Age 5-8. | Audience: K to
    grade 3. | Includes bibliographical references and index.
Identifiers: LCCN 2016052719 (print) | LCCN 2017013855 (ebook) | ISBN
    9781626176140 (hardcover : alk. paper) | ISBN 9781681033440 (ebook)
Subjects: LCSH: Newfoundland dog–Juvenile literature.
Classification: LCC SF429.N4 (ebook) | LCC SF429.N4 S66 2018 (print) | DDC
    636.73–dc23
LC record available at https://lccn.loc.gov/2016052719

Editor: Betsy Rathburn   Designer: Kathy Petelinsek

Printed in the United States of America, North Mankato, MN.

Table of **Contents**

Newfoundlands are huge dogs known for being smart and strong.

They are gentle, friendly helpers. People often call them Newfies.

Newfies have large heads with wide **muzzles**. They have small, dark eyes.

← muzzle

Newfie ears look
like triangles with
rounded tips.

Strong Bodies and Double Coats

These dogs have big, strong bodies. They can weigh up to 150 pounds (68 kilograms).

Webbed paws and muscular legs make Newfies excellent swimmers.

Newfies have heavy double **coats**. Soft, thick fur lies beneath a rough outer coat.

Newfoundland Coats

brown   black   white with
                         black

Newfies can be brown, gray, or black. Some are white with black markings.

History of Newfoundlands

Newfies are from Newfoundland, an island in Canada. They have been around for **centuries**.

Newfoundland

N
W E
S

They likely come from dogs
owned by European fishermen.

Newfies have always been hard workers. Some owners first used them to pull fishing nets and haul wood.

Others used them to rescue
people from water.

In the 1800s, paintings by Sir Edwin Landseer helped make the **breed** popular.

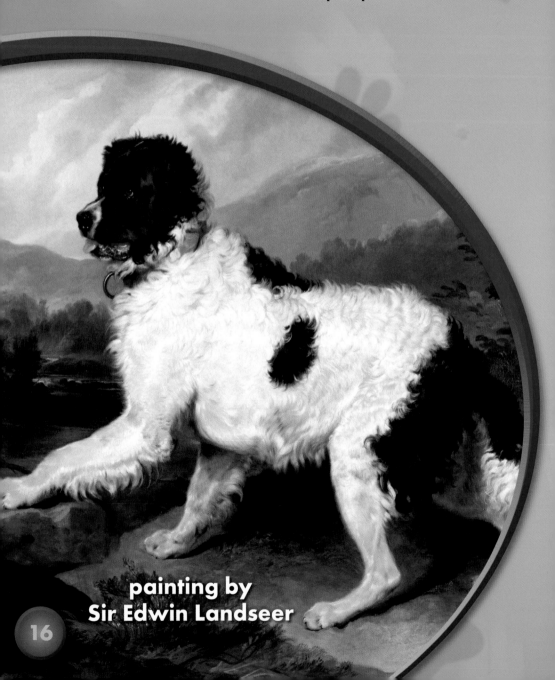

painting by
Sir Edwin Landseer

Newfoundland Profile

large body

heavy double coat

webbed paws

Life Span: 8 to 12 years

Trainability:

| 1 | 2 | 3 | 4 | 5 | 6 |

Hardest to train   Easiest to train

In 1886, Newfies joined the **American Kennel Club**. They are part of its **Working Group**.

Today, Newfies still love the water. They also make great **companions** for hikers.

Owners must be careful in hot weather. Newfies' thick coats cause the dogs to **overheat** easily.

These big dogs are sweet and
lovable. They are **patient** with
children and strangers.

Newfies are **loyal** family pets!

Glossary

American Kennel Club—an organization that keeps track of dog breeds in the United States

breed—a type of dog

centuries—hundreds of years

coats—the hair or fur covering some animals

companions—friends who keep someone company

loyal—having constant support for someone

muzzles—the noses and mouths of some animals

overheat—to become too hot

patient—able to stay calm in difficult situations

webbed paws—paws with thin skin that connects the toes

Working Group—a group of dog breeds that have a history of performing jobs for people

To Learn More

AT THE LIBRARY
Bluemel Oldfield, Dawn. *Newfoundland: Water Rescuer*. New York, N.Y.: Bearport Pub., 2012.

Landau, Elaine. *Newfoundlands Are the Best!* Minneapolis, Minn.: Lerner, 2011.

Morey, Allan. *Newfoundlands*. North Mankato, Minn.: Capstone Press, 2016.

ON THE WEB

Learning more about Newfoundlands is as easy as 1, 2, 3.

1. Go to www.factsurfer.com.

2. Enter "Newfoundlands" into the search box.

3. Click the "Surf" button and you will see a list of related web sites.

With factsurfer.com, finding more information is just a click away.

Index